Don't Ask
for the
Dead
Man's Golf
Clubs

"Don't Ask

What to Do and Say

for the

(and What Not to)

Dead

When a Friend

Man's Golf

Loses a Loved One

Clubs"

BY LYNN KELLY

Workman Publishing • New York

Library of Congress Cataloging-in-Publication Data
Kelly, Lynn.
   Don't ask for the dead man's golf clubs: what to do and say (and what not to) when a friend loses a loved one / by Lynn Kelly.

      p. cm.
   ISBN 0-7611-2186-2

   1. Grief. 2. Bereavement—Psychological aspects. 3. Death—Psychological aspects. 4. Loss (Psychology) I. Title: What to do and say (and what not to) when a friend loses a loved one. II.Title
BF 575.G7K44 2000
155.9'37—dc21   00-044777

Cover design by Paul Gamarello
Interior design by Linda McCarthy
Spot illustrations by Shelly Bartek
Back cover photo by Mikel-Gamber Photography/Aurora, CO

Workman Publishing Company, Inc.
708 Broadway
New York, NY 10003-9555
www.workman.com

Manufactured in the United States of America

First Printing August 2000

10   9   8   7   6   5   4   3   2   1

TO PETER

ACKNOWLEDGMENTS

My sincere, heartfelt thanks to all of the people I interviewed for taking time to remember and revisit often very painful memories and for sharing the experiences that made this book possible.

I would also like to thank Carl Larson, Jeanne Lesem, Darrell Mayabb, Eric Evert, Joe Betts, and most especially, Michael Psaltis for your extra effort, Margot Herrera for your thoughtful editing, and my ace associate Mary Kay Mauro for all of your help and encouragement. Finally, to Ryan, Leslie, Chris, Ginge, and Mom: thank you for never losing faith in me.

CONTENTS

INTRODUCTION

Coping with death is never easy. It comes at all the wrong times to all the wrong people—to parents who lose precious babies, to newlyweds and lifelong couples, to favorite brothers and only sisters. It may be expected or sudden, through every imaginable illness or by suicide, murder, or terrible accident. Even the deaths of those who say they are "ready to go" are no easier for the grieving families and friends left behind.

When the bereaved is a good friend, it can be very difficult to know what to say or do to bring him or her some measure of comfort.

I was widowed at a relatively young age (34), left with three small children, and have since lost my father and many other family members. As a result of these experiences, I learned some fairly specific things to say and do to comfort a friend in a time of loss.

As the years passed, I found myself consulted more and more often by my friends about what to say or do when death claimed someone close to them. This little book began as a guide to help friends know what to say and do to help a friend who has lost a loved one.

I have come to believe that the people best qualified to make suggestions are those who have themselves lost an immediate family member. With that in mind, I conducted in-depth interviews with survivors who had lost husbands, wives, children, mothers, fathers, brothers, sisters, grandmothers, and grand-fathers. They talked about what their friends did, in the first few weeks after the death and over time, that helped them. They also talked about what did not help.

The people I spoke with ranged in age from 17 to 90. They lived across the United States and in Canada, in tiny rural towns, middle-sized cities, and major metropolitan areas. They lost their loved ones to disease, suicide, stillbirth, and accidents.

Their incomes ranged from near nothing to extreme wealth. They represented a variety of ethnicities and races. They were religious people and those who practiced no faith. They were farmers, entrepreneurs, mechanics, nurses, lawyers, homemakers, retirees, insurance agents, students, executives, secretaries, teachers, administrators, librarians, salespeople, small-business owners, artists, and managers. They were our neighbors, our friends.

This book summarizes their thoughts and feelings. What is instantly clear is how kind friends are to one another. I am in constant awe of the wondrous things friends do for friends, in words and deeds so straight from the heart they seem effortless, although I know better.

In some instances, the names of the interviewees have been changed to protect their privacy.

I am neither a counselor nor a psychiatric expert, and this book is not intended to offer professional advice to the bereaved or their families. It is meant to provide friends of the bereaved some practical ideas on how to comfort their friend, and, in so doing, to receive a little comfort for themselves.

What to Do Now

BE THERE

There is no question that being there for your friend is the best thing you can do immediately after a death. Sometimes we are so afraid we will do or say the wrong thing that we stay away. This is the worst thing to do, because it sends a message that you don't care. Get in your car, or on the plane, train, or your bike, and go to the home for a visit, even if you only stop by for a few minutes. There is no substitute for your physical presence. One of our best friends got in his car at 4 A.M. and drove two hours to be with me the morning Pete died. Because he was with me, I knew he cared.

"Go over to the house. Give them a hug and tell them you are sorry. Take off your hat and coat and look around. See what needs to be done."

> Mary K. McLaughlin, Torrington, WY
> *Husband, Joseph, 69, heart failure*

◆

"If they had not been here, I think I would have felt like I had lost my friends. It was very important to me that they be here."

> Fannie Booker, Hattiesburg, MS
> *Husband, Leonard W., 83, pneumonia*

◆

"It bothered me if they did not come."

> Phil Dineen, Denver, CO *Mother, Margaret, 71, cancer*

◆

"The best thing friends can do is be there, and when I say that, I mean spend time in the home with the people who are mourning."

> Rabbi Bruce Greenbaum, Carmel, CA
> *Brother, Brian, 30, complications of AIDS; father, Norm, 59, blood disorder*

If you live too far away from the bereaved to make a personal visit, call or write. If your friend has to leave town to be with the family, find a way to reach him or her and express your sympathy. Knowing you have the support of your friends when you are far away is a big lift.

"I was in Atlanta for several months with my dad. I was so lonely, but I got nearly one call a night to keep me sane and in touch with my friends at home."

Joan McKnight, Littleton, CO
Father, Alton, 79, cancer; mother, Ruth, 79, Alzheimer's disease

◆

"As soon as I got home, I was overwhelmed by the support of my friends and so many cards and flowers."

Valerie Tracy, Minneapolis, MN *Mother, Wanda, 59, cancer*

Even if it has been a long time since you last spoke to your friend, it is better to do something than to do nothing. It isn't how much time has gone by that's important. The message that you care is what counts.

> "If you haven't been in touch for awhile, that's okay. We get busy with our own lives and we forget. But friends are forgiving. This is not like talking to the bank when you've missed a payment. If you haven't been in touch for awhile, pick up the phone and call. Say, 'How are you? I'm thinking about you.' Your friend will forgive you."
>
> Gary Massaro, Denver, CO *Father, Angelo, 81, natural causes*

GO TO THE SERVICE

It is important to the whole family to see you at any services held. It sends a valuable message of support.

"Take off work, even if you are busy, and go to the
funeral. It just means an awful lot to look out and
see how many people cared about the person you
loved, and care about you."

Sandra C. Dillard, Denver, CO *Mother, Ruth, 91, stroke*

◆

"Seeing how full the church was of people who loved
and cared about her helped."

Robin Teske, Torrington, WY
Sister, Shelly, 17, killed by a drunk driver

◆

"I was 13 and I was almost overjoyed to see my
friends at my mother's wake. I didn't think any of
them cared."

Scott Chojnowski, Rocky River, OH
Mother, Dorothy, 40, multiple sclerosis

If you aren't able to attend the service, let the
family know you are thinking about them at
that time.

"I knew I couldn't go to Spokane to my uncle's funeral, so I called my aunt and asked what day the service was going to be held. I told her I would go to church here on that day."

Gerry Cummins, Littleton, CO
Uncle, Ermin, 69, heart attack

◆

"My friends were out of state and couldn't come, so they had a service on the same day within an hour of when we had Ryan's service. They had flowers, they played the recording of what our oldest son was going to say, and had a complete service just as though we were there. It was mind-boggling that they did that for us, for Ryan."

Becky Sciba, Kent, WA *Son, Ryan, 19, cancer*

WHAT TO SAY

We worry about the right thing to say, but more important than the actual words is letting your friend know that you genuinely share in his or her sorrow. Be honest, but don't go overboard. Simplest is usually best.

"What you say has to come from the heart. People should be sincere, but not gushy."
Ron Hines, Littleton CO *Father, George, 91, heart failure*

◆

"Say, 'I am sorry for your pain. I am here to support you. I am here to help you in any way I can.'"
Karen Lee, Littleton, CO *Husband, Gerald, 52, suicide*

◆

"Say, 'I am sorry a life is gone. He was a dear person and I'm sure you're going to miss him.'"
Loretta Ukulele, Denver, CO *Husband, Harry, 92, cancer*

"Say, 'We were really fond of him and we remember the good times we had together. He was important to us.'"

  Peter Resler, Englewood, CO
  Brother, Tim, 26, complications of AIDS

◆

"Try to say something. Even if you cause tears, it's better to say something than not to say anything."
  Bob Coates, Exeter, Ontario, Canada *Brother, Jim, 52, cancer*

◆

"In Boston, where I'm from, we express our sympathy with these simple words, 'I'm sorry for your trouble.'"
  Jackie Campbell, Denver, CO
  Mother, Dorothy, 92, natural causes

◆

"My friends just said, 'We're here for you.'"
  Josh Strittmatter, Patton, PA *Brother, Jeff, 23, suicide*

"The Japanese Buddhist way is to say, 'How lonely
you must be.' It hits to the core of our being."
Okamoto Kanya, Denver, CO
Father, Masao, 84, birth (the cause of death in Buddhist tradition)

If you think "I'm sorry" could be misinter-
preted (for example, if the person who died
has been ill or in pain for a long time), qualify
what you mean.

"When the dearly departed had been suffering or ill,
it is comforting to consider they are no longer
suffering, and to recognize the illness was an ordeal.
So say, 'I'm so sorry you and your loved one have
had to go through all this. Who shall I call to see
what I can do?'"
Ellen Kelly, Seattle, WA *Mother, Ruth, 84, leukemia*

Let the bereaved tell you how he or she feels
about the loss or suffering first. Don't start
out by telling your friend what you think.

"I know it was for the best. I realized that he was so much better off. But it is much better that I say it first."

Fannie Booker, Hattiesburg, MS
Husband, Leonard W., 83, pneumonia

◆

"Nobody said it was a blessed relief more than I did, but I should be the one who says it first. Then you can agree with me. It may be a blessed relief for the person who died, but not for the living. They are sad. Let them tell you how they feel."

Allie Coppeak, Vail, CO *Husband, Bill, 60, cancer*

Talk about the person who died. Share your fond memories. Don't be afraid to say his or her name because you think saying it will cause pain. The pain is already there.

"We needed to talk about our little boy and how precious he was."

Ann Griggs, Abilene, TX *Son, Allen, 17 months, car accident*

"Tell them what a wonderful person she was and talk about her achievements and how she did things for you and funny things that happened when you were together."
Sam Newton, Englewood, CO
Daughter, Deborah, 7, home accident

◆

"It is great to hear stories about the person who died and to have friends let you know how much they liked and appreciated your loved one."
Marge Druckman, Potomac, MD
Father, Norbert, 61, cancer; mother, Jean, 72, Alzheimer's disease

◆

"When Dad's friends told me stories about him, it made me feel good that his life meant something not just to me but to other people, that he contributed to other lives. It let me see a part of my dad I didn't know."
Josh Densberger, Washington, DC
Father, William, 47, helicopter accident

Express sympathy to all of the family members. If you don't know them, introduce yourself and explain your relationship to the person who died.

> "It's important to offer condolences not just to the widow or widower, but to grandma and everyone else."
>
> Ginger McLaughlin, Torrington, WY
> *Father, Joseph, 69, heart failure*

◆

> "Let all the people who are grieving know how important the deceased was to you and then just be there."
>
> Ed Mahr, Albuquerque, NM
> *Father, Edwin, 65, Alzheimer's disease; mother, Mary Winifred, 84, complications of a broken hip*

Be honest. If you don't know what to say, don't be afraid to say so.

"If you are not comfortable, tell the person, 'I've never experienced this before, and I don't know what to say.' Don't avoid it."
 Lianne Enderton, Calgary, Alberta, Canada
 Brother, Darcy, 32, unknown causes

Y ou might not need to say anything. Actions can speak louder than words.

"An old, old friend of my dad's came by. He couldn't talk. He just put his hand to his heart and gave me a hug. That was all he needed to do."
 Gary Massaro, Denver, CO *Father, Angelo, 81, natural causes*

"Our best friends were there physically for five days. They didn't have to say anything."
 Gary Olson, Torrington, WY
 Son, Michael, 14, boating accident

"A friend of my mother's came over to the house. She didn't say anything. She just sat down on the couch and held Mom's hand."

Blenda Crawford, Littleton, CO
Sister, Cindy, 21, car-train accident

◆

"I don't think it makes any difference what people say. It is just the idea that they are there and you know they care."

Diana Redmond, Memphis, TN
Mother, Esther, 80, heart failure

INCLUDE CHILDREN

The hardest thing I ever did in my life was wake my children and tell them their father had died. We cried together for a long time. They wanted to know what happened and to talk about their dad, to hold on to their memories of him. They also needed to know what to do—to see that it was okay to be sad, to cry, and be angry, to know that his death was not their fault.

Let children see your sorrow. Be honest and reassure them, but don't deny the severity of the situation. It also helps to understand that children grieve, and, like adults, need to go through the grieving process to heal. I cannot stress enough what a gift it is to tell children fond stories about the person they lost.

"I would give every thing I have for one memory of my father."
    Chris Kelly, Bloomfield, NJ *Father, Peter, 38, heart failure*

◆

"It was the most help when people talked to us about her, so it was less scary to think we would forget her because we were so young."
    Sarah Minifie, Cambridge, MA *Mother, Lola, 42, leukemia*

"I wanted to talk about my dad. My memory was all I had left. I was eight years old and I was so lonely. I thought the terrible feeling would last forever. Reassure the children that they are strong and they will get through it. If you don't understand what they are going through say so, but don't b.s. them."
Ryan Kelly, Santa Monica, CA *Father, Peter, 38, heart failure*

◆

"I was eight when my mother died. I remember all of a sudden realizing a huge crowd of people was in the house and not knowing what was happening. Finally, somebody took me aside and told me what was going on. I think it is best to try to be as truthful as you can with children. They wonder and worry and they need to have some understanding on their own level."
Mark Cohen, Morris Plains, NJ
Mother, Rose, 33, hypertension; father, Abner, 85, stroke

"Let children see you grieve so they know it is okay to cry and they can cry, too."
  Marge Lee, Long Island, NY
  Son, Kenny, 25, killed by a drunk driver

◆

"I wrote a speech when I was in middle school about how I can change tomorrow. It was for the next little kid whose father had died, and it said, 'Here's my shoulder, come and cry on it.'"
  Joel Bershok, Littleton, CO *Father, Gerald, 52, suicide*

◆

"We felt it was very important for the children to go through the grieving process with us. I think struggling through the pain with them, seeing me on days when I just cry, will make them stronger as they grow. They don't see me as made of stone."
  Mary Rindone, Omaha, NE *Son, Nicholas, stillborn*

If you offer to help children, mean it. After my husband died, every guy that came over told my older son he would take him fishing. It never happened, and my son never forgot.

> "I can't tell you how many men said, 'We'll be there for the boys. They'll need a man around.' But they never came."
> Karen Lee, Littleton, CO *Husband, Gerald, 52, suicide*

IT'S OKAY TO CRY

Don't worry about trying to hold back your tears. It helps the bereaved to know that their friends are sad, too. They can find comfort knowing their friends care enough to cry. It confirms that the person they lost meant something to others, too.

> "If they are really, really close friends, it is strange for them not to cry in front of you."
> Sarah Minifie, Cambridge, MA *Mother, Lola, 42, leukemia*

"I never realized you feel comfort in the fact that others could share in your sorrow."
Lianne Enderton, Calgary, Alberta, Canada
Brother, Darcy, 32, unknown causes

◆

"It is kind of nice when your friends cry with you."
Penny Hutchins, Harrisonburg, LA
Mother, Edna, 79, cancer

Expect the bereaved to feel bad. If they start to cry, let them. It is a needed release.

"Don't be afraid if the bereaved cry. Say, 'That's all right' and don't try to stop them from crying. It is okay to cry with them, too."
Marge Lee, Long Island, NY
Son, Kenny, 25, killed by drunk driver

◆

"Being able to share the grief seems to lessen it. Everyone who feels your pain takes a little of it. They help you carry it. It wasn't enough to know

that I loved her. I needed to know that others loved
and missed her, too."

    Patty Lou Wood, Torrington, WY
    Daughter, Shelly, 17, killed by a drunk driver

Touch your friend. Hugs are good. If your
friend is not open to a hug, touch his or her
hand. If your friend shrinks back from a hug,
just let go.

"Shake hands and say something nice about the
person who died. The physical touch is good. Give
them a hug."

    Rich Mauro, Littleton, CO
    Father, Joe, 68; mother, Mary, 65, both of cancer

◆

"Give them a hug and say, 'I'm really sorry for what
happened to you.'"

    Rona Cohen, Morris Plains, NJ *Three babies, miscarried*

IT'S OKAY TO LAUGH

There's a myth out there that somehow laughter is inappropriate at this time. That's not true. Finding humor in a fond memory of the person who died and sharing it eases the pain and helps us heal.

"You need some humor because there's such a lump in your chest and it's the only thing that softens it for awhile."

Donna Phipps, Lingle, WY *Husband, Lloyd, 39, cancer*

◆

"Humor is invaluable. Utterly invaluable. That's how you survive."

Ed Mahr, Albuquerque, NM
Father, Edwin, 65, Alzheimer's disease; mother, Mary Winifred, 84, complications of a broken hip

◆

"It helped to cry and laugh at funny stories that are fond memories."

Brad Mikel, Aurora, CO *Wife, Betsy, 44, cancer*

"My brother's nature was one of humor, love, and happiness. We found so much comfort in telling funny, silly stories about him. He would have enjoyed them. Laughing keeps the lid on the teapot. It helps us cope."

Diana Gaston, Bigfork, MT
Brother, Raymond, 25, auto accident

Laughter doesn't mean disrespect for the dead.

"One of Shelly's friends heard us laughing. She was so mad about it, she left. I went and talked to her and told her we weren't making fun of Shelly, we were sharing happy memories. I told her it was okay to laugh."

Patty Lou Wood, Torrington, WY
Daughter, Shelly, 17, killed by a drunk driver

"The Irish have a fine tradition. You can tell stories at the wake, laugh and cry and tell jokes and it is not at all offensive. It isn't disrespectful to the person who died or to their spirit. They would want you to laugh with them."

Dan Guthrie, Elizabeth, CO *Wife, Lisa, 30, suicide*

◆

"Humor is really important. It is healing to laugh."

Ruby Mercer, Palm Springs, CA *Husband, Poddy, 78, cancer*

◆

"Laughter is very healthy in a mourning situation. Remembering the person at their best times when they made people happy and made them smile makes us laugh and helps heal some of the pain. It is not a time of comedy, but the full range of memories should include when the person who died made us laugh, made us smile, made us feel good."

Rabbi Bruce Greenbaum, Carmel, CA
Brother, Brian, 30, complications of AIDS; father, Norm, 59, blood disorder

"Laughter to me is most important because I know deep in my heart that my son would not want to see me crying."
  Mary Martinez, Denver, CO *Son, Clint, 18, fatally shot*

KNOW WHEN TO LEAVE

Respect your friend's need for privacy. Although it is a great comfort to have friends there, time alone is also necessary. Sometimes I needed to be by myself to rest, think about what had happened, and sort through my options or just to weep and howl my pain.

"Even though you're around, you have to give them space. Know when you can help and when you are in the way. Don't be a buttinski with what the family is deciding."
  Ginger McLaughlin, Torrington, WY
  Father, Joseph, 69, heart failure

"Sometimes I just needed to be alone to sort things out and process."
Lis Brown, Denver, CO
Husband, Tony, 49, Hodgkin's disease

◆

"You have to try and tune into the person's feelings and body language. If they start to look remote and glassy-eyed, that's the time to cut the visit a little shorter than you had planned."
Rona Cohen, Morris Plains, NJ *Three babies, miscarried*

WHAT TO WRITE

Send a note, letter, or telegram, or a card with a handwritten note expressing your sorrow. It feels good to know your friend cares enough to write something, even if it is only a few words.

"It wasn't necessarily what they said. It was that they took the time to write. It was a comfort to know

they were thinking of you, that you had friends and people who loved you and wanted to talk to you."

Francesca Amberto, Cambridge, MA
Father, Nicholas, 64, riding accident

◆

"The most important things were the notes I received from dear friends who knew my husband. I still have them."

Joan Wright, Franklin, LA
Husband, John, 64, natural causes

◆

"Cards are great. Some of the things people wrote were awesome. They showed how mom had touched people and made a difference in the world. You knew deep down her life was meaningful to them."

Phil Dineen, Denver, CO *Mother, Margaret, 71, cancer*

"I offer my sincere sympathy. I say that I join them in their sorrow, and that I feel for them and just hope they don't feel like they are all alone in their grieving."

   Flotilde Hammack, Front Royal, VA
   Mother, Erlinda, 53, jaundice

◆

"I write, 'I am thinking of you at this difficult time' or 'I am praying for you at this difficult time' if I know that they are religious. It is good to draw parallels. Sometimes I write a short letter that says, 'I understand. As an only child with both parents gone, I know how fragile life is right now.'"

   Joan McKnight, Littleton, CO
   Father, Alton, 79, cancer;
   mother, Ruth, 79, Alzheimer's disease

◆

"I keep blank note cards so I can write something right away. I know if I wait to buy a card I might forget or put it off. I just jot a quick note. I say, 'My thoughts and sympathy are with you. I am sure your

dad was proud to have a daughter like you,' or I say,
'Just a note to let you know I'm thinking of you.'"
   Gerry Cummins, Littleton, CO
   Father, Roman, 75, complications of diabetes

◆

"If I didn't know the person who died, I write how sorry
I am that I never got a chance to know him or her."
   Kathy Moriarty, Torrington, WY
   Brother, Mike, 18, skin-diving accident

Write a fond memory of the person who
died. I liked it when people wrote me
cards with stories about my husband. I saved
them so the kids could read about their dad.

"Any piece of history shared about Tony was
   important to me. I wanted to know what his co-
   workers thought of him, stuff he never told me—
   his sense of humor, his creativity, the special
   qualities that made him unique. That was a
   tremendous help and a record for the kids, too."
   Lis Brown, Denver, CO *Husband, Tony, 49, Hodgkin's disease*

"The most moving cards were those from people who took the time to write a story."
Brad Mikel, Aurora, CO *Wife, Betsy, 44, cancer*

Send a picture of the person who died. Photos can show a side of the person or a time in his or her life that the family might not know or remember.

"The pictures people sent of my mom when she was young helped me."
Chris Evers, Denver, CO *Mother, Dorothy, 44, cancer*

Write notes on special days—birthdays, holidays, anniversaries, and especially the anniversary of the death.

"I was afraid I would not remember to send cards, so in my tickler file I always put a bunch of postcards and just write, 'Have a happy day' or 'Thinking of

you' and send them so my friend will always have something on the holidays."

Elizabeth Montaño, Santa Fe, NM
Husband, Robert, 38, killed by a reckless driver

Help your child make a card for his or her bereaved friend.

"Little Clark went every day to the mailbox. He was waiting for a card addressed to him from his sixth-grade class. It was his personal card, and they all had signed it. It meant the world to him."

Jane Wisniewski, Scottsbluff, NE
Father, Clark, 70, heart failure

◆

"I was seven when dad died. The first day we went back to school my sister's whole class had gotten her a present and made her a card. They all signed it. I wished that had happened to me."

Becky Galardi, Omaha, NE *Father, Seymour, 48, cancer*

Send an e-mail or an electronic postcard.

"The people from work sent me e-mails. I don't remember the words, but I'll never forget the sentiment."

Gary Massaro, Denver, CO *Father, Angelo, 81, natural causes*

Here are some additional suggestions of what to send with your card or letter:

- Ask if there is a preferred charity and send a contribution in the name of the person who died.
- Ask if there is a special fund for the children or the family, and if so, send a contribution.
- Enclose extra stamps with your letter or sympathy card. Save your friend a trip to the post office when writing thank-you notes.

- Enclose long-distance calling cards or long-distance gift certificates with your letter or card. The family can use them to notify and keep in touch with relatives and friends who are far away.
- If the family is Catholic, you may want to enclose a Mass card.

PITCH IN AND HELP

Ordinary chores are the last thing on the minds of the bereaved. Taking care of any everyday job around the home is a huge help. Get a notebook and make a list of things that people can do when they call and ask how to help. Don't be afraid to tell them that somebody needs to drive or baby-sit or bring in a pizza or do whatever is needed.

When the children and I came home from being out of town at my husband's funeral, we found a full pantry, refrigerator, and freezer, a complete stock of cleaning and laundry supplies and a house so spotless that a friend remarked, "Your kitchen floor is so clean that if a flea tried to cross it he'd break all his arms and legs." All sorts of little repairs had been done, and there was a note on the kitchen counter that said, "Welcome home. Dinner is in the refrigerator and we have taken care of the rest of the meals for the week. Love, Your Neighbors." I will never forget their kindness.

"Our families are far away from where we live. Now, our friends are our extended family. I do for my neighbors and friends what I would do for my family. It is important to help each other."
Gerry Cummins, Littleton, CO
Father, Roman, 75, complications of diabetes

Assist with visitors and calls. Answer the door and the telephone. Keep a record of who called and what was said. Make sure somebody is around.

"People came and stayed at the house when we had to go to the funeral home. Somebody needs to do that."
Judy Banister, Torrington, WY *Father, George, 86, cancer*

◆

"A volunteer from hospice went back to the house, turned on the lights and the radio and made coffee so it wouldn't be dark when the family got home."
Linda Rock, Scottsbluff, NE
Father, John, 51, car accident;
mother, Hazel 71, aortic aneurysm

Let your friend rest if possible.

"If the widow is asleep and somebody calls or comes over, don't wake her up. It might be the only rest she's been getting for a week."
   Ginger McLaughlin, Torrington, WY
   Father, Joseph, 69, heart failure

Organize a phone tree to notify friends and co-workers.

"Friends took shifts answering the phone. They organized a phone tree to notify people in organizations my wife belonged to."
   Dan Guthrie, Elizabeth, CO *Wife, Lisa, 30, suicide*

Screen phone calls for telemarketers.

"The last thing I wanted to hear was a salesperson asking for my husband."
Allie Coppeak, Vail, CO *Husband, Bill, 60, cancer*

O ffer to help your friend when he or she wants to record a new phone message.

"It is hard to take your husband's voice off the message machine."
Kathryn Halpin, Denver, CO
Husband, Steve, 69, pneumonia and acute respiratory distress syndrome; mother, Dorothy, 69, cancer

I f relatives need a place to stay, help find places for them or offer beds at your home. Also, help arrange transportation. Offer to pick up people from the airport, bus, or train station, and offer to give them a lift to the funeral, too. If they have transportation, they still may not know their way around. Draw a map or give directions. Also, remember that the bereaved may not be able to drive because of their grief. It's hard to drive when you are crying.

"Make motel reservations for out-of-town visitors."
Ellen Kelly, Seattle, WA *Mother, Ruth, 84, leukemia*

◆

"Offer to drive them to the viewing so they can cry."
Bob Buffington, Aurora CO
Father, Bob, 74; mother, Rose, 75, both of stroke

◆

"Offer to drive the family to pick out the headstone."
Ryan Kelly, Santa Monica, CA
Father, Peter, 38, heart failure

◆

"Offer to drive to the social security office to fill out benefits paperwork."
Kathryn Halpin, Denver, CO
Husband, Steve, 69, pneumonia and acute respiratory distress syndrome; mother, Dorothy, 69, cancer

Keep track of donations, flowers, and food items and who brought what.

"Write down what kind of flowers were sent so you don't write and say thank you for the chrysanthemums when they sent azaleas."
   Dan Guthrie, Elizabeth, CO *Wife, Lisa, 30, suicide*

◆

"Take snapshots of flower arrangements that are delivered and note who they are from."
   Jill Austen, Littleton, CO
   Daughter, Julie, seven weeks, heart failure

◆

"Generally speaking, flowers are always nice, but if you aren't sure whether to send flowers, call and ask."
   Carmen Piceno White, Westminster, CO
   Brother, Ray, 60, complications of pneumonia

Ask if the family needs help with funeral arrangements. Many people have family members to help with the arrangements for burial and services, but if family is not around, it is a great help to have a friend to lean on.

"My godfather planned the funeral and okayed it with all of us. It was helpful not to have to do that."
Jean Christopher, Medina, OH
Mother, Peggy, 49, hit by a car

◆

"Offer to drive to the mortuary and stay around to remind your friend that she doesn't have to buy everything they suggest."
Jill Austen, Littleton, CO
Daughter, Julie, seven weeks, heart failure

Assure your friend that any funeral or burial arrangements he or she makes are just fine.

"A lot of people worry about putting a funeral together in the right way. Tell them not to worry.

It will be just fine. Hopefully, we won't ever get very good at it."
    Bob Buffington, Aurora, CO
    Father, Bob, 74; mother, Rose, 75, both of stroke

Help with the obituary if the family is not available.

"Help put a thank-you in the newspaper if it is customary. Help pay for the ad."
    Ginger McLaughlin, Torrington, WY
    Father, Joseph, 69, heart failure

If you have expertise in an area where your friend needs help, offer it.

"Say, 'Let me help you. I know about social security,' or 'I know about insurance.' I worked in a bank and for years I've been helping a widow who didn't know how to balance her checkbook."
    Sandy Van Heukelem, Denver, CO
    Husband, Ron, 32, brain hemorrhage

Help with clothing. Ask if you can go to the nursing home or hospice and pack the belongings of the person who died. Or offer to help the family get ready for the service. If necessary, run a load of wash and get out the iron. If it's necessary, take family members shopping for something to wear to the funeral, or for other needs.

What if they don't have anything to wear? Ask, 'Do you want me to go shopping with you?'"
> Jill Austen, Englewood, CO
> *Daughter, Julie, seven weeks, heart failure*

◆

"Press clothes that the family will wear. See that children have clothes ready."
> Marge Lee, Long Island, NY
> *Son, Kenny, 25, killed by a drunk driver*

Treat your friend to a trip to the barber or hairdresser.

> "My hairdresser called and said, 'I'm not sending flowers, but I'd like to give you a color, cut, and set instead.' I thanked him for making me look better than I felt during a difficult time."
> Kathryn Halpin, Denver, CO
> *Husband, Steve, 69, pneumonia and acute respiratory distress syndrome; mother, Dorothy, 69, cancer*

Find the "to do" list. All homes have jobs that need doing. Find them and do them. For example, you might donate a housekeeper or clean the house yourself. You might lift or move heavy items, or fix things that need repair. Remember seasonal jobs. Shovel the walk, clean the porch, patio, or deck. Rake the leaves. Care for the garden.

"A young woman came in and did the dishes. Nobody asked her to do it, but she saw it needed to be done. I will always remember that."
Judy Banister, Torrington, WY *Father, George, 86, cancer*

◆

"Friends came in and organized the kitchen. They cleaned the refrigerator. They fixed things. I couldn't think of that stuff."
Boni Fullmer, Casper, WY *Husband, Rod, 51, suicide*

◆

"Mow the lawn because that's the farthest thing from your mind when this is happening. Just don't mow over the flowers."
Brian Wells, Chadron, NE *Father, Lloyd, 39, cancer*

Don't forget the pets.

"Pets need comforting, too. Walk the dog, pet the cat, clean the cage, feed the bird."
John McCoy, Key West, FL
Daughter, Sylvia, 26, complications of AIDS

Care for vehicles. Wash the car. Take the car in for service and/or winterizing.

"It's nice to make recommendations about car service. I had oil coming out of the car and it was helpful to have someone tell me it was not going to be a big repair job, just a valve, and to give me an idea of what the labor cost would be."
   Fannie Booker, Hattiesburg, MS
   Husband, Leonard W., 83, pneumonia

◆

"I helped my friend out with new tires for her car. It was out of respect for her husband that I did it. He would have done the same for me."
   Gary Olson, Torrington, WY
   Son, Michael, 14, boating accident

HELP YOUR FRIEND
FEEL SAFE

Make sure your friend doesn't feel nervous about being alone. Stay over or help find someone reliable to stay at the home. Let your friend know it's okay to call you anytime. Make a list of emergency numbers and put them near the phone.

"Buy your friend a cell phone and arrange for free emergency service so he or she can call 911 from anywhere."

Kathryn Halpin, Denver, CO
Husband, Steve, 69, pneumonia and acute respiratory distress syndrome; mother, Dorothy, 69, cancer

BRING FOOD

Bringing food is almost always a good idea. It relieves the burden of meal planning, shopping, and cooking and sends a thoughtful message. Take simple, nutritious foods as well as comfort foods. It's great if the dishes you bring can be frozen.

"If I tried to pay people back for what they did for us, I never could. They washed our clothes, they brought in food. If they hadn't, I would never have eaten anything."
   Ann Griggs, Abilene, TX *Son, Allen, 17 months, car accident*

◆

"Plan meals. Fill in what people have brought with other items."
   Robin Volk, Cheyenne, WY
   Father, Jack, 66, horseback riding accident

"The bereaved often aren't hungry so take food that is easy to eat, like little sandwiches or pizza. Sneak in some nutritious snacks like vegetables or fruit."
Ginger McLaughlin, Torrington, WY
Father, Joseph, 69, heart failure

◆

"Cinnamon rolls smell so good. They're homey and warm and give you that deep down, roots-are-still-there feeling, the feeling that life can still be good without saying any of that."
Donna Phipps, Lingle, WY *Husband, Lloyd, 39, cancer*

Call and ask what kind of food is needed or what they have plenty of already.

"When we got the fifth ham I started to laugh."
Sam Newton, Englewood, CO
Daughter, Deborah, 7, home accident

If possible, take food in containers that need not be returned.

"If you want storage or serving dishes returned, make it easy for your friend. Put a self-stick address label or a piece of masking tape with your name on it on the bottom as a reminder."
 Jeanne Lesem, New York, NY
 Father, Henry, 51; mother, Jeanette, 82, both of cancer

If you are not a cook, find someone who is.

"If you can't cook, don't bring food."
 Phil Dineen, Denver, CO *Mother, Margaret, 71, cancer*

Be aware of special or religious diets.

"Don't take a ham to a kosher Jewish home."
 Carol Hull Barnett, Champaign, IL
 Father, Jack, 66, horseback riding accident

"Call and ask if anyone has special dietary restrictions. For example, if you know that someone in the family has high blood pressure, take a dish without salt."

Joan McKnight, Littleton, CO
Father, Alton, 79, cancer; mother, Ruth, 79, Alzheimer's disease

◆

"Take a vegetarian dish."

Leslie Kelly, Washington, DC *Father, Peter, 38, heart failure*

Put a note on the dish describing what it is and giving cooking directions.

"We took a dish out of the freezer and we had no idea what it was. Is this a dessert or a main dish? Shall we cut it up or put it in the oven? We took a chance and let it thaw."

Lianne Enderton, Calgary, Alberta, Canada
Brother, Darcy, 32, unknown causes

Give store-prepared dishes a personal touch.

"If you are too busy to cook, stop at the deli and buy some macaroni and cheese. Take 15 minutes to take it out of the plastic, put it in an attractive container and toast some buttered bread crumbs to sprinkle on top."

Robin Volk, Cheyenne, WY
Father, Jack, 66, horseback riding accident

Arrange to have meals delivered.

"The office took up a collection and had meals delivered for two weeks. The caterer brought lunch and dinner, and they always came with a flower on the tray."

Mary Voelz Chandler, Denver, CO
Husband, David, 60, suicide

If there are lots of visitors at the home, make sure they have what they need. Find or rent a large coffeemaker and take it to the home.

Consider picking up plastic forks, paper plates, napkins, and disposable cups as well as household items like paper towels, laundry and dishwasher detergent, soap, toilet and facial tissue. If there are lots of people around, you might want to bring folding chairs.

"I wish someone had rented a large coffeemaker for me and brought over a can of coffee."
Ellen Kelly, Seattle, WA *Mother, Ruth, 84, cancer*

♦

"I try to bring something useful like bread, rolls, butter, cold cuts, or something that doesn't have to be fussed over, and I usually take paper towels, napkins, and toilet tissue."
Flotilde Hammack, Front Royal, VA
Mother, Erlinda, 53, jaundice

CULTURAL CONSIDERATIONS

Families observe many different traditions at the time of death. The ideas that follow are not intended to cover the myriad of customs that exist in our culture, but rather to suggest that you may find your friend dealing with death in a different way than your own.

Some families prefer large gatherings where people drink beer and tell stories. Others favor a small, private observance. Still others choose to do nothing. Some families display photographs at the funeral of the person who died. Others photograph the dead person in the casket. Regardless of how different from yours the tradition may be, your role as a friend does not change. You are there to support and help. If you don't know what is appropriate for you to do, ask. Your friend will be happy to guide you.

Generally speaking, services are published in the newspaper so friends can attend. Although different faiths observe different traditions, friends of different beliefs are usually welcome. For example, Catholic tradition includes a prayer service or rosary the night before the funeral Mass, both of which are open to non-Catholics. Also, visits to the home are appropriate.

In the Jewish tradition, friends are invited to offer moral support to families observing *shiva,* the seven-day period of mourning. It is not necessary to be Jewish to attend. If the family is of the Islamic faith, the ideal time for visiting may be during a period of three days after the burial. It is best to call and ask when you can visit.

Often families enclose cash or checks with a sympathy card as a helping gesture. If you are attending a Japanese Buddhist or Japanese

Christian funeral, for example, it is customary to bring an envelope with your name on it containing money. A table will be provided for the envelopes. The money is used to help pay for the funeral, and the family will send you a thank-you.

Condolences often are accompanied by flowers. Flowers are lovely and usually are much appreciated. They are a visible reminder that people care, and they bring life and beauty into the home. However, sometimes flowers may not be the best gift. The Jewish tradition, for example, de-emphasizes sending flowers and stresses finding ways to help the family by bringing food and offering support. In the Islamic faith, sending flowers could convey the message that you are glad the family lost that person. Some families prefer donations to a charity or special fund in lieu of flowers. Also, some people may be allergic to certain plants and flowers.

If you are in doubt about whether or not to send or bring flowers, check with the family.

What to Do over Time

The flurry of activity dies down, and the day arrives when everybody who has been there for a week or two leaves. The shock starts to wear off, and the reality of the loss sets in. It is in this confusing and lonely time that friends really count, and when being there as a friend is not always easy. Things will never be the same, so expect your friend to change. Your friend may pull away or act quite differently toward you. Be patient. Your friend needs time to get better. He or she also needs your support as much as ever.

Just as there is no time limit on grief, neither is there any time limit on these suggestions.

"Without my friends, I would never have made it."
Becky Sciba, Kent, WA *Son, Ryan, 19, cancer*

LISTEN

This is the number-one thing that a friend can do to help now. When your friend is ready to talk, he or she needs a willing and sympathetic ear, and will need it often. Be patient. You could be listening for a long time. When I was ready to talk, I talked nonstop for two years, pretty much repeating myself the whole time. My sister, who patiently listened, should be canonized.

"Listen, even though you've heard it a million times. You don't have to say anything. Just listen. Ask questions. Ask what kind of person she was."
Sandra C. Dillard, Denver, CO *Mother, Ruth, 91, stroke*

"If the bereaved person wants to talk, let him or her talk and say the same thing over and over. You have to talk it out of your system. Even if it is monotonous or boring or grisly, it is the healing process. Friendship, like parenthood, is not always about the good times. You have to listen, even if they are driving you nuts."

Dorothy Clark, East Stroudsburg, PA *Son, Darby, 26, suicide*

◆

"My friends allowed me to express myself. I thought her death was unfair. I've been an evil, wicked, mean shagnasty and lived a full life. Why her and not me? It's important to say those things out loud to someone, not just let them bounce around in your head."

John McCoy, Key West, FL
Daughter, Sylvia, 26, complications of AIDS

Remember that asking you to listen does not mean asking for your advice.

"Just listen. If they want to be angry, let them. If they want to feel sorry for themselves, let them. Don't get all high and mighty and tell them how they should be feeling. They don't need your advice. They have to come to conclusions on their own."
Chris Kelly, Bloomfield, NJ *Father, Peter, 38, heart failure*

B e a safe listener. Respect your friend's feelings and keep his or her confidences to yourself.

"I needed a safe place to go and talk about my mom with someone who treated me like an adult."
Sarah Minifie, Cambridge, MA *Mother, Lola, 42, leukemia*

◆

"I was afraid to tell too much. I thought, 'Is this going to be all around the school the next day. Is it safe to cry?' "
Joel Bershok, Littleton, CO *Father, Gerald, 52, suicide*

Let your friend lead the conversation.

"My wife likes to talk about it. I don't. I think you should let the person lead the way, not try to lead them. People have totally different ways to grieve."

Gary Olson, Torrington, WY
Son, Michael, 14, boating accident

◆

"What was helpful were the people who let me ramble when I wanted to ramble and let me go at my own pace, because I went in waves."

David Kelly, Springfield, VA
Brother, Brian, 25, killed by a drunk driver

"If I want to talk about it, fine. If I don't, that is fine, too."

Ruby Mercer, Palm Springs, CA *Husband, Poddy, 78, cancer*

HELP REMEMBER

Reminisce with your friend. Continue to tell fond stories about the person who died. We want to talk about our loved one. A memory is a wonderful gift to give your friend.

"A big complaint from victims is that their friends stop talking about the person who died because they're afraid it will hurt the living. Just the opposite is true. It is a comfort when somebody says, 'This is Kenny's birthday. It must be a tough day.'"
Marge Lee, Long Island, NY
Son, Kenny, 25, killed by a drunk driver

◆

"It is wonderful to hear from people about who my father was."
Susan Coppeak, Littleton, CO *Father, Bill, 60, cancer*

"I like to talk about him to bring back the good times
and put the best memories in my head."
Josh Strittmatter, Patton, PA *Brother, Jeff, 23, suicide*

◆

"The most comforting things to me now are hearing
stories about my dad's love of life—how he could
turn lemons into lemonade. I am very, very proud of
his accomplishments, so it's a good feeling when I
stumble across someone who really knew my Dad
and hear them chuckle while they reminisce."
Becky Galardi, Omaha, NE *Father, Seymour, 48, cancer*

◆

"I love to remember anything at all about Ryan and
to bring it up. 'Oh, he used to do this.' I want to
hear every single thing that anyone can remember
about him—any funny thing, anything, because I
don't know all the interaction he had with others. I
want to keep him alive with the memories.
Otherwise he is a picture and that's it."
Becky Sciba, Kent, WA *Son, Ryan, 19, cancer*

"One of the most comforting things a friend did was to tell me how much I look like my mother. It was a wonderful thing to say. It means there is still a part of her in me, and I liked that."

Penny Hutchins, Harrisonburg, LA
Mother, Edna, 79, cancer

◆

"What we liked best is what the minister said at Dad's funeral. We put it on his headstone. It was, 'As long as we remember, we are all together.'"

Sarah Williams, Scottsbluff, NE
Father, Clark, 70, heart failure

Don't worry that it will cause pain to talk about the person who died. Actually, the reverse is true—it hurts more to think that people don't remember or no longer care.

"It's not going to hurt to talk about the person. The damage has already been done. What's bad is to ignore what happened. It drives me crazy that people would assume that my dad's not a part of my life."

Josh Densberger, Washington, DC
Father, William, 47, helicopter accident

◆

"I think that people don't ask about the dead because they think it will hurt you. But it helps to talk about them. It helps keep them alive. I want to talk about them."

Bunny Mayer, Littleton, CO
Granddaughter, Marta, six months, Down's syndrome

◆

"One friend said how good it made her feel that I had acknowledged the death of her teenaged daughter, and consequently her life. Many people had just avoided mentioning her daughter, Liz, at all. Although I'm sure their reasoning was not to

open wounds, not mentioning her really made the wounds more painful."
    Lesley Bartlett, Torrington, WY
    Grandmother, Helen, 92, heart failure

LEARN ABOUT GRIEF

Do your best to learn about the grieving process and how people go through different stages over time. A classic book on this topic is Elisabeth Kübler-Ross's *On Death and Dying.* Remember that everyone grieves in his or her own way and time. Don't be like the person who got mad because his mother and sister weren't over their grief after six weeks. Instead, be like my neighbor who read up on grief and could assure my children that I was behaving normally when I was disbelieving, angry, forgetful, depressed, withdrawn, or when I inexplicably burst into tears.

Be patient. Expect your friend to say and do odd things. I once began to cry when I turned on the garden hose. I have no idea why.

"I know I repeat myself. I don't remember where I'm supposed to be. It is wonderful to know that is normal and I'm not crazy."
Kathryn Halpin, Denver, CO
Husband, Steve, 69, pneumonia and acute respiratory distress syndrome; mother, Dorothy, 69, cancer

◆

"Things come out of your mouth that you don't mean."
Boni Fullmer, Casper, WY *Husband, Rod, 51, suicide*

◆

"You can't think straight, that's all."
"Dutch," Paw Paw, MI *Wife, Mona, 61, brain aneurysm*

Reassure your friend that what he or she is feeling is normal.

"When they break into tears at a song, I tell them I understand."
> Brad Mikel, Aurora, CO _Wife, Betsy, 44, cancer_

◆

"Let them know it's okay when they're feeling anger and abandonment."
> Brian Wells, Chadron, NE _Father, Lloyd, 39, cancer_

Reassure your grieving friend that he or she will make it through.

"I told my friend, 'Just keep on keeping on.' She said it was the best thing I could have said."
> Robin Volk, Cheyenne, WY
> _Father, Jack, 66, horseback riding accident_

E xpect your friend to heal, but not to get over it. There is no timetable on grief. We just learn to live with it.

"I hope I don't ever get over it. Then he really would be gone forever."
Leslie Kelly, Washington, DC *Father, Peter, 38, heart failure*

◆

"It's like waves in the ocean. At first they come one after another, crashing down on you. Later they don't come as often, but when one comes, it hits you just as hard."
Tom Stevens, Denver, CO *Son, Eric, 27, suicide*

◆

"I miss my dad to this day, the way he would have dealt with situations."
Tracy Ringolsby, Parker, CO *Father, Tracy, 60, kidney failure*

◆

"I don't think it will ever end for me because there will always be times when I won't have my dad."
Josh Densberger, Washington, DC
Father, William, 47, helicopter accident

"It's not like the chicken pox."
    Mary Lou Williams, Scottsbluff, NE
    Husband, Clark, 70, heart failure

W hen you ask, "How are you?" don't
    expect your friend to say "Okay."

"When people said, 'How are you doing?' I wanted
to say, 'How in the hell do you think I'm doing. I
am alone. I miss going home and having somebody
there, somebody to touch. We did everything
together.' Instead say, 'Hi, it's good seeing you. I've
been thinking about you.' "
    John Peterson, Lingle, WY
    Wife, Virginia, 44, cancer

◆

"Doing good does not mean that you are going out
partying. Doing good means you are up off the
couch. If you're not lying there, relying on pills and
alcohol all day, you're doing okay."
    Barbara Cleaver, Torrance, CA
    Son, Scott, 26, complications of AIDS

Expect your friend to continue to cry.

"Occasionally I just lose it, thinking about that little
boy I don't have."

Ann Griggs, Abilene, TX *Son, Allen, 17 months, car accident*

◆

"To this day, when I start thinking and reminiscing,
the tears start all over again. I don't find that to be a
bad thing. I guess I feel good about the fact that I do
feel that way and I still miss them."

Joe Nicolich, Franklin Square, NY
*Wife, Janice, 60; granddaughter, Robyn, 11, both killed by a
drunk driver*

◆

"When we were working on the music in church my
tears were rolling and the girl next to me was
crying, too, because she knew exactly what was
going on. My friends there just reached out and
touched me and said, 'I know and I am here.' "

Ann Odom, Memphis, TN
Husband, James H., 62, pulmonary embolism following surgery

"My dad celebrated the beginning of each season
with the fruit of that season. Long after he died,
there I was, a grown woman at the fruit department
in the grocery store, crying like somebody was
running over my foot."
Kristeen Tadich, Bellevue, NE
Father, Dimitri, 74, lung disease

CHECK IN OFTEN

The months and years after losing a loved
one are very lonely. Let your friend know
you are thinking about him or her. Check in
regularly. Call and say, "Hi, what are you doing
today?" or "I'm thinking about you and I
thought I would give you a call." Driving alone
can continue to be a problem for the bereaved.
Keep an eye on your friend and be there if he or
she needs a lift. Take your friend to look at
security systems if he or she is apprehensive

about being alone in the house or apartment.
Ask if you can help find a watchdog.

> "I think everybody is guilty of leaving people alone too
> much. You think that you should call, but you don't."
> Jo Ann Williams, Tillsonburg, Ontario, Canada
> *Father, John "Jack," 69; sister, Lil, 38, both from cancer*

> "Now that I am alone, nobody knows if I wake up in
> the morning or not. I need a phone call in the
> morning so somebody knows I am alive."
> Kathryn Halpin, Denver, CO
> *Husband, Steve, 69, pneumonia and acute respiratory distress
> syndrome; mother, Dorothy, 69, cancer*

◆

> "Let me tell you, bereavement is not for sissies. I
> wondered what would become of me. I was all

alone. I went through a period when I thought I was going to be a bag lady. It was terrifying. I'll never forget when an old school friend said, 'You'll never have to worry about not having friends or being a bag lady. We will always have a place for you.' "

Liz Stevens, Las Vegas, NV
Husband, Edward, 34, complications of AIDS

◆

"The women in the church office in the town where my dad lives fix extra meals for him to take home for dinner. They invite him to a lot of family things, too. They really have adopted him. It makes me feel so much better when I am living far away."

Diana Redmond, Memphis, TN
Mother, Esther, 80, heart failure

Stop by for a visit.

"Just be company. When you lose a father or a spouse, you are so lonely. Just being company helps."

    Brian Wells, Chadron, NE *Father, Lloyd, 39, cancer*

◆

"Just giving encouragement, being concerned and coming by and keeping us company did a lot for us."

    Piedad Mary Arebalo, Amarillo, TX
    Father, Luis, 64, brain aneurysm

◆

"A lot of his friends still come over and call to see how we are doing. They visit and talk about things they used to do with Clint and we all laugh and cry together. I hope this will go on for a long time."

    Mary Martinez, Denver, CO *Son, Clint, 18, fatally shot*

◆

"My mother's friends knew my brother and I were away in different cities. I will always be grateful to everyone who made that extra effort to provide her with company and to let her know they were there for whatever, whenever. I will never forget what they did for my mom."

Mary Wu, Williamsburg, VA *Father, Jerry, 49, cancer*

Offer to help dispose of clothing and personal items if family is not available.

"Someone needs to be there with you to think about things like checking the pockets."

Diana Boutwell, Parker, CO
Father, Steve, 69, pneumonia and acute respiratory distress syndrome

Invite your friend to do things. Be specific about the plans.

"Instead of saying, 'Let's do lunch,' say, 'Let's do lunch Tuesday,' and do it until their life takes them off in a different direction. They won't need you to do it forever. They will take off and you can be happy for them when they change."

Donna Phipps, Lingle, WY *Husband, Lloyd, 39, cancer*

Tell your friend it is okay not to go.

"My friends kept inviting and inviting me and they never stopped. I could say no and that was okay. Sometimes I didn't want to go out."
Boni Fullmer, Casper, WY *Husband, Rod, 51, suicide*

◆

"Let them set the pace on going places and doing things. Let them judge when they should or shouldn't do things. Respect their choices. Everybody does it differently. It is important to go at their pace, not at your pace."
David Kelly, Springfield, VA
Brother Brian, 25, killed by drunk driver

Let widows or widowers know if it is a singles or couples event. It is hard to be the only single at a couples event if you aren't prepared for it. Understand if your friend is not comfortable.

"That first year it was very hard for me, especially
the social things. So many times there was dancing.
I would disappear and my friends understood."
   Ruby Mercer, Palm Springs, CA
   Husband, Poddy, 78, cancer

Mealtime can be lonely. Invite your friend
to eat with you. My neighbors still invite
me over for dinner when they know I am alone.

"After awhile the phone quits ringing. Remember to
call on your way home. Say, 'Why don't you stop in
for dinner' or 'We're having family night and we
want you to come over' or 'We'd like to take you to
dinner.'"
   Dan Guthrie, Elizabeth, CO *Wife, Lisa, 30, suicide*

◆

"The hardest part is at mealtime when no one is
there."
   Jean O'Hara, Cambridge, MA
   Husband, Tom, 63, heart failure

"The thing I hate is eating alone. It's funny, when I traveled it was okay. I ate a lot of meals by myself. But that wasn't at home."

Hal Shroyer, Westminster, CO *Wife, Maxine, 79, cancer*

Bringing food is still a good idea.

"The grieving don't eat for weeks and months. Make something and leave it on the porch or call and say, 'I'm bringing dinner over tomorrow night.'"

Ginger McLaughlin, Torrington, WY
Father, Joseph, 69, heart failure

◆

"My neighbors still bring casseroles. I like having them come and eat with me."

Paul Silent, Littleton, CO
Son, Timothy, 29, complications of AIDS

Weekends are tough. It is a time when families do things together. Give your

friend a call. Invite him or her to a movie.
Think of something to do together.

> "Sundays were terrible, so I called my friends and
> organized a bridge game on Sunday afternoon."
> Mary K. McLaughlin, Torrington, WY
> *Husband, Joseph, 69, heart failure*

◆

> "Married people didn't seem to realize how
> devastating the weekends were."
> Lis Brown, Denver, CO
> *Husband, Tony, 49, Hodgkin's disease*

Help your friend make new memories.
Encourage him or her to try something
new. Hang in there even if your friend doesn't
respond to your first idea, or second, or third.

"My dad is so lonely since my mom died. We are helping him to work on projects, go to sporting events, try bingo, or anything that will help."
    Patty Congdon, Littleton, CO
    Mother, Betty, 76, cancer

◆

"If one thing doesn't work, try something else."
    Shirley Weaver, Denver, CO
    Son, Dan, 30, complications of AIDS

◆

"Say, 'Let's go for a walk' or 'Let's play some hoops.' If one out of ten times the person goes to play basketball with you, that's good. It's not a remedy to all their problems, but they might feel a little better. Don't give up on a friend."
    Chris Kelly, Bloomfield, NJ *Father, Peter, 38, heart failure*

Continue to treat your friend like a friend. If you're worried that talking about your child or parent or spouse is going to be painful for the person who just lost someone, ask, "Is it uncomfortable or painful for you to hear stories about my mother?" Your friend will tell you if it is okay, or if it hurts too much.

> "Some things will be different, but really try and be the same way with the person. It's important to hang out, to ask, 'Why don't we go have a beer or some dinner?' Don't exclude us."
> Josh Densberger, Washington, DC
> _Father, William, 47, helicopter accident_

REMEMBER HOLIDAYS

Holidays are miserable. Around the holiday season, try to make sure that your friend isn't alone.

> "The first Christmas we went to Vermont and met new people and had a new family tradition with another family."
> Sarah Minifie, Cambridge, MA _Mother, Lola, 42, leukemia_

"We went to a holiday party and coming home all of a sudden I started to cry. It was because everyone there had their mothers with them."

Sue Chojnowski, Lakewood, OH
Mother, Dorothy, 40, multiple sclerosis

Remember your friend on the little holidays like birthdays, Mother's and Father's Day, Valentine's Day, graduations, weddings, and all the celebrations that will be held without the person who died.

"I still miss my mother and it has been close to thirty years. On Mother's Day I wish I had a mother to send one of those pretty cards to."

Flotilde Hammack, Front Royal, VA
Mother, Erlinda, 53, jaundice

"It's important to call and ask how your friend is doing, especially on Father's Day and other holidays."

Paul Silent, Denver, CO
Son, Timothy, 29, complications of AIDS

A cknowledge the anniversary of the death. It is a sad time, always.

"It's important to realize this is a tough day and you need a little extra support."

Gail Lee Sander, El Paso, TX *Husband, Richard, 42, cancer*

◆

"One friend just looked at me and said, 'Hard times, huh.' It meant more than if she had said something flowery."

Barbara Cleaver, Torrance, CA
Son, Scott, 26, complications of AIDS

"There is a lovely Jewish tradition called *Yarzheit,* the word for lighting a candle on the anniversary of someone's death and allowing it to burn until it goes out."

Janet Elsbach, Sheffield, MA *Baby miscarried, three months*

◆

"Within our Buddhist tradition we have a funeral, then we have *HoJi* or teaching thing for the living to remember our loved ones who have died. We have *HoJi* on the seventh day after the death, the forty-ninth day, the hundredth day, and on the first, third, seventh, thirteenth, seventeenth, twenty-fifth, and fiftieth years."

Okamoto Kanya, Denver, CO
Father, Masao, 84, birth (the cause of death in Buddhist tradition)

HELP WITH THE KIDS

It is hard to ask for things and it is hard to remember who said, "Let me know what I can do." I was working after my husband died and since I had three kids, it seemed like I always needed help to get them to their soccer games and piano lessons. I hated to have to keep asking my friends to help. It was just wonderful when somebody would offer and I didn't have to ask. Offer not only to drive the children, but to take them for a weekend. Offer to watch the kids in the summer and after school. Think about what would be helpful with children, now and later.

"People figured out that because we had no mom we needed certain things. They would take us to shop for tampons without having to be asked. They would remember to do things like that."
Sarah Minifie, Cambridge, MA *Mother, Lola, 42, leukemia*

"My mom's best friend has been wonderful since the day it happened. She never forgets my birthday. She would see me or meet with me for lunch at least once a week until I got married. She helped me plan my whole wedding. We drove to Pittsburgh to help me find a wedding dress and ran all over town."

Jean Christopher, Medina, OH
Mother, Peggy, 49, hit by a car

◆

"My dad always used to tell me how he would protect me. After he died I felt that protective barrier had slipped away. One day my best friend and I were talking about some guy we were oogling over and her dad said to her, 'If I ever see you with him I will kick you in the butt.' Then he looked at me and said, 'That goes for you, too.' Saying that meant a lot to me. It meant I had that father figure. Fathers always talk about having to chase the boys away."

Terri Ouellette, Phoenix, AZ *Father, Bob, 54, heart failure*

KEEP GIVING HUGS

I used to go down to the Denver Press Club because I knew that everybody there would hug me and I needed that. I still do.

"The thing I missed most was touching, not sexual touching, just physical touching. Hug 'em and hug 'em and hug 'em."
Donna Phipps, Lingle, WY *Husband, Lloyd, 39, cancer*

◆

"Hugs and listening are good forever."
Shirley Weaver, Denver, CO
Son, Dan, 30, complications of AIDS

◆

"The thing I missed most was being held. I just wanted somebody to put their arms around me."
Sandra C. Dillard, Denver, CO *Mother, Ruth, 91, stroke*

LITTLE THINGS COUNT

Caring doesn't have to be a big production. It's the little things friends do that you keep close to your heart.

"One of his friends, a marine with ties to Vietnam, came over and polished Tony's sword."
Lis Brown, Denver, CO *Husband, Tony, 49, Hodgkin's disease*

◆

"A year after my mother died my friend sent me a big bouquet of flowers with a card that said, 'Thinking of you on your mother's first birthday in heaven.' "
Kathryn Halpin, Denver, CO
Husband, Steve, 69, pneumonia and acute respiratory distress syndrome; mother, Dorothy, 69, cancer

◆

"Ryan loved children, and now there are three little Ryans named after him. That is really nifty."
Becky Sciba, Kent, WA *Son, Ryan, 19, cancer*

"I find a little angel ornament and take it to the mom to put on the tree. The first Christmas a girlfriend did that for me. She said, 'This is a little Scott angel.'"

Barbara Cleaver, Torrance, CA
Son, Scott, 26, complications of AIDS

◆

"A friend sent me a package that said, 'Keep your senses alive, don't let them shut down.' It was hand lotion, potpourri, candles, and a book about care of the soul."

Mary Voelz Chandler, Denver, CO
Husband, David, 60, suicide

◆

"Bill is buried in Texas. His secretary takes a plant there for every holiday, his birthday, Father's Day, and Christmas. She never told me about it, but she does it and has been doing it for 15 years."

Allie Coppeak, Vail, CO
Husband, Bill, 60, cancer

"A friend gave us an orchid that will live forever as long as we take care of it. It means the world to me."

Seth Kaufman, Brooklyn, NY *Son, Jonah, stillborn*

◆

"One of our friends had a tree planted in Harry's name."

Loretta Ukulele, Denver, CO *Husband, Harry, 92, cancer*

◆

"A little boy Dan had met at the fire station colored a sad clown and sent it to our family with a note that said how happy he was that Dan had been in his neighborhood, and how sad he was to learn that Dan died because he was so kind and strong. The fire department hand-delivered that picture and note and the graduation photo of Mayor Daly handing Dan his firefighter's badge."

Theresa Soloma, Chicago, IL *Son, Dan, 24, car accident*

"The hospital gave me a beautiful box all decorated on the outside and filled with all sorts of things from the baby: a tiny hat, a little blanket, a wrist band, the name card with his name, weight, and length and the little shell the priest used to baptize the baby. It is a little treasure of remembrances."
Mary Rindone, Omaha, NE *Son, Nicholas, stillborn*

◆

"His friends go out to the cemetery every weekend, and my baby always has flowers, fresh flowers."
Mary Martinez, Denver, CO *Son, Clint, 18, fatally shot*

What Not to Do

Friends sometimes say things to the grieving that are well-meaning but inappropriate. They may not mean to be offensive, but they are, and it hurts. Following are some suggestions of things to be avoided.

"People say things without thinking. You forgive them, but you never forget."
Bob Buffington, Aurora, CO
Father, Bob, 74; mother, Rose, 75, both of stroke

DON'T BE JUDGMENTAL

Don't judge the way in which your friend grieves. We all grieve in our own way, in our own time. Some people cry. Others do not. If your friend isn't crying, it doesn't mean that he or she is not sad or is unfeeling. We may not know the reason. What's important is to be supportive, regardless.

"It took me five years to cry. Don't judge the person who is grieving just because that is not how you would grieve, unless they're being self-destructive."
  Brian Wells, Chadron, NE *Father, Lloyd, 39, cancer*

◆

"I was fourteen and I felt strange because I wasn't crying all the time. I think the reason I felt that way was that people had the expectation that I should be more visibly emotional. The tears actually came much later but at the time I was not very emotive. I remember even the parents of my friends being critical, asking 'Why aren't you crying?' and 'Why aren't you upset?' then feeling bad about myself and not understanding why."
  Carol Starkey, Boston, MA *Mother, Angela, 40, cancer*

"If you're not crying, it doesn't mean you're cold-hearted. When my wife's folks died, I couldn't show emotion. I was taking care of her. It was probably six months later before I could deal with it myself. You have to find a time and place."

Ron Sentz, Midlothian, TX *Father, Mike, 88, heart failure*

◆

"What gets me is people who say, 'Oh, she's not holding up well,' if you're crying; but if you're not crying, they say, 'Oh, I don't think she's faced up to it.'"

Sarah Williams, Scottsbluff, NE
Father, Clark, 70, heart failure

R espect the family's choices. Don't criticize the arrangements. What's important is what the family deems appropriate.

"It might not be the way you would do it, or what you would want, but let it go. If it is comforting to them, let them do it without saying anything."
    Judy Banister, Torrington, WY *Father, George, 86, cancer*

◆

"Don't make judgments if there is not a funeral. It is a family choice."
    Tom Cummins, Littleton, CO *Mother, LeEtta, 75, cancer*

AVOID ASSUMPTIONS

Don't push your beliefs on the bereaved. Whatever you believe is fine, but your friend may very well hold a different view. For example, don't say, "It's God's will."

"People express sympathy and say it is God's will that it happened. I just can't believe that. When you get some drunk that kills them, it's not God's will."
    Joe Nicolich, Franklin Square, NY
    Wife, Janice, 60; granddaughter, Robyn, 11, both killed by a drunk driver

"Nobody better say that to me."
  Shirley Weaver, Denver, CO
  Son, Dan, 30, complications of AIDS

◆

"I don't like phrases like that. Are you telling the
  person that they didn't want their loved one as
  much as God did? When the person has suffered
  tremendously, I say that I am glad the person is not
  having to suffer anymore, but I know it is always
  painful for those left behind."
  Rabbi Bruce Greenbaum, Carmel, CA
  *Brother, Brian, 30, complications of AIDS; father, Norm, 59,
  blood disorder*

Don't assume they think it's for the best or
that it's in any way a blessing.

"Our granddaughter had Down's syndrome and died
  during an operation when she was six months old.
  We loved her just the same as if she had been
  perfect. And it hurt just as much."
  Bunny Mayer, Littleton, CO
  Granddaughter, Marta, six months, Down's syndrome

"When she heard I lost my baby, one woman said, 'It is probably for the best.' It was not for the best. It was my baby."

    Sarah Campbell, Denver, CO
    Baby Emma, miscarried, 8 weeks

◆

"It's no blessing. Nor did it matter if he was healthy or sick. He was my dad."

    Jane Wisniewski, Scottsbluff, NE
    Father, Clark, 70, heart failure

◆

"What saying that does is underscore his removal from the grieving person and their care. He didn't want to die. He had the kids and their future ahead of him. Acknowledge reality and don't smooth it over with Victorian sentiments. Say, 'I know this is going to be hard for you.' "

    Lis Brown, Denver, CO
    Husband, Tony, 49, Hodgkin's disease

DON'T MINIMIZE THE PAIN

Don't assume that because there are no children, the pain is any less.

"People say, 'Well thank God they didn't have any children,' as if not having any children made the person expendable. That's not true. It is just a different set of problems."
Jane Wisniewski, Scottsbluff, NE
Father, Clark, 70, heart failure

Don't assume that because there are other children, the pain is any less.

"Don't say, 'Well, you still have the children.' If I lost a leg, I would still miss that leg."
Gary Massaro, Denver, CO *Father, Angelo, 81, natural causes*

"One person said, 'At least you have four other children.' What? Like I had a litter and I gave one away?"

>   Marge Lee, Long Island, NY
>   *Son, Kenny, 25, killed by a drunk driver*

◆

"When I went back to work one person said, 'It can't be that bad. At least you have other brothers and sisters. I looked at him and said, 'Just wait until you have a couple of kids, then you try and figure out which one you can do without.'"

>   Blenda Crawford, Littleton, CO
>   *Sister, Cindy, 21, car-train accident*

Don't assume that the pain is any less because the person who died was older or very ill.

"People ask how old she was and then say, 'Oh well, seventy-nine' like if she were a child it would be different."

>   Hal Shroyer, Westminster, CO *Wife, Maxine, 79, cancer*

"I didn't want my mom to be the way she was. But no one wanted to give up. If you get hit by a truck it doesn't matter whether you see it coming or not. It is no less a blow."

Phil Dineen, Denver, CO *Mother, Margaret, 71, cancer*

AVOID COMPARISONS

Don't say, "I know how you feel" no matter what your experience has been. The relationship I had with my husband was unique to the two of us, just as the relationship each person has with the person he or she has lost is unique. No one else can know those feelings.

"People say, 'I know just exactly what you're going through,' but they don't know. We had been married for sixty years and all of a sudden I am alone."

Lorraine Sweeney, Torrington, WY
Husband, Ron, 87, heart failure

"The thing I didn't like was when people said, 'I know how you must feel losing a brother.' They didn't at all know that."

Derek Sciba, Seattle, WA *Brother, Ryan, 19, cancer*

Don't fall into grief one-upmanship. Some people will say that the loss of a child, for example, is the worst kind of loss. It is terrible to lose a child. But it is also terrible to be a child and lose a parent. Or to lose your partner of 60 years. Or the brother you grew up adoring. All loss hurts.

"You can't compare hurt. I don't know how someone else feels. It just hurts and I don't ever try to measure it."

Ann Griggs, Abilene, TX
Son, Allen, 17 months, car accident

Don't make parallels with animals.

"Don't ever say, 'I know it's not the same, but I can really empathize because I lost my dog.' "
Becky Sciba, Kent, WA *Son, Ryan, 19, cancer*

◆

"One person came up and said, 'Are you going to get a dog now?' I couldn't believe it. Did they think I could replace my husband with an animal? That any warm body would do? I will never forget it."
Mary Voelz Chandler, Denver, CO
Husband, David, 60, suicide

WATCH WHAT YOU SAY

There is no replacement for the person who died. Don't say, "Don't worry, you'll get married again."

"I was still grieving for my husband and it made me mad when people said it."

    Elizabeth Montaño, Santa Fe, NM
    Husband, Robert, 38, killed by a reckless driver

◆

"That's like saying, 'Don't worry. This pair of shoes is worn out now, but they have them on sale, just about the same model.' "

    Kathryn Halpin, Denver, CO
    Husband, Steve, 69, pneumonia and acute respiratory distress syndrome; mother, Dorothy, 69, cancer

◆

"I never thought I would ever want to be with anybody else."

    Jean O'Hara, Cambridge, MA
    Husband, Tom, 63, heart failure

D on't say, "Don't worry, I'm sure you'll have another baby."

"It doesn't make you feel any better. You can't replace someone who died. I didn't want another baby later. I wanted my baby now."
   Elaine Reeves, Denver, CO
   Sons, Michael and Nicholas, stillborn

D on't say unkind things about the person who died, or air old grudges.

"What is not helpful is someone who remembers a negative story and shares it. One woman made a remark about how difficult my father was. It made me mad. If you don't have something nice to say, keep your mouth shut."
   Kathy Smith, Dallas, TX
   Father, John, 72, lung disease

D on't preach.

"The grieving don't want to be talked at. They want to have a discussion. The clergy seems to understand this when they speak to the grieving."

David Kelly, Springfield, VA
Brother, Brian, 25, killed by a drunk driver

D on't imply that the person who died deserved to die.

"It made me so mad when some holier-than-thou said, 'If she hadn't been that way, God wouldn't have struck her dead with AIDS' or 'It was just a purification thing.' I wanted to pulverize them."

John McCoy, Key West, FL
Daughter, Sylvia, 26, complications of AIDS

◆

"You have to look at every person as if he or she were your brother or your child when a loved one dies. Judgment has no place, no matter what the situation."

Diana Gaston, Bigfork, MT
Brother, Raymond, 25, auto accident

ADJUST YOUR EXPECTATIONS

Don't force behaviors on the bereaved. For example, don't make your friend feel guilty if he or she doesn't go to other funerals. I couldn't go to a funeral for years. It was too painful. I just told my friends it hurt too much. Likewise, don't make your friend feel guilty for not attending church.

Remember that it's hard to go back to the same places and do the same things when a person you love is missing from the picture. It was horrible to return to my husband's favorite restaurant with friends and sit at a table for six with one chair empty. Don't push your friend to go to the same places and do the same things he or she did before.

"It's hard to go to church and live through the hour of quiet time when you are thinking about your baby. I spent many Sundays in church crying and nobody knew why I was crying."

Jill Austen, Englewood, CO
Daughter, Julie, seven weeks, heart failure

◆

"I can't go to a football game at the high school. It hurts too much."

Gary Olson, Torrington, WY *Son, Michael, 14, boating accident*

Don't push alcohol.

"Don't urge them to drink. Booze is a depressant and you still have to wake up the next morning by yourself."

Boni Fullmer, Casper, WY
Husband, Rod, 51, suicide

"It is your job as a friend to act as a chaperone. It is not your job to go and get drunk with the family. The wake is not a free drunk for you. This is a time for you to be a social drinker, maybe sip one or two, but be there to watch out for your friend."

Gary Massaro, Denver, CO
Father, Angelo, 81, natural causes

DON'T ASK FOR GIFTS

Don't ask for money or gifts. It sends a message that somehow their loss is your gain. On the way home from Pete's funeral, somebody was already sounding me out for some cash, asking how much money my husband left. When they are ready, the family will offer what they want to give.

Instead of asking for gifts, find ways *you* can give. Make sure the survivors are financially okay. Start a scholarship fund for the children.

"My dad had four tickets on the Nebraska forty-five-yard line, twelve rows up. He used to say he wouldn't be cold before somebody would ask for those tickets. He was right. His funeral was on Wednesday and that afternoon the phone rang and a guy said, 'I'm sorry about your dad. By the way, what are you girls going to do with those football tickets?'"

Sarah Williams, Scottsbluff, NE
Father, Clark, 70, heart failure

◆

"Bill had a nice golf cart. The day of the funeral the phone rang and a man said, 'Oh, I am so sorry about your husband. I didn't want to call today but I was afraid I would miss you and I wanted to ask if you are going to sell Bill's golf cart.' I couldn't believe it."

Allie Coppeak, Vail, CO *Husband, Bill, 60, heart failure*

"Darcy had a lot of really nice golf clubs. You can't believe how many people called and asked if they could have them."
Lianne Enderton, Calgary, Alberta, Canada
Brother, Darcy, 32, unknown causes

◆

"My son had a pet python. We got a call from someone who barely expressed sympathy, just said, 'I'll take the snake.' Instead, I called the Chicago Herpetological Society and will never forget how enormously kind the representative was. He sent us a picture of Stinky in his new habitat and wrote how he was really a she and would be laying eggs soon. He said because Dan had taken such good care of her, she would be taken around to schools."
Theresa Soloma, Chicago, IL *Son, Dan, 24, car accident*

STICK BY YOUR FRIEND

It is terrible when your friends desert you. Suddenly, people you've known for years never call again. You have no idea why. You just know how much it hurts. You're not only faced with coping with your loss, but also with finding new friends. If being around the family is a too painful reminder that your close friend has died, tell the family why you're not there. It will help them understand.

"I wonder why people desert you. Just because I am not a couple anymore doesn't mean we can't get together."
Brad Mikel, Aurora, CO *Wife, Betsy, 44, cancer*

◆

"I think that you shouldn't end a friendship during the grieving. You might not agree with what your friend is doing, but the grief is so powerful that you should try to hang in there until he or she gets well. So when they get mad or deny God or do all of that, you are still there for them."
Ginger McLaughlin, Torrington, WY
Father, Joseph, 69, heart failure

"I had two girlfriends I had gone to high school with. We got together and they asked if Edward had died from complications of AIDS. When most people would pull away from me, they gave me hugs."
Liz Stevens, Las Vegas, NV
Husband, Edward, 34, complications of AIDS

LAST BUT NOT LEAST

D on't visit the bereaved if you are out of control. Crying is okay. Hysteria is not. Things are already tough enough on the bereaved without expecting them to provide professional help.

"One person was hysterical and screaming and it put me on edge. She wanted me to take care of her, and I could not do it."
Boni Fullmer, Casper, WY *Husband, Rod, 51, suicide*

"One of our friends would call me and say her husband just couldn't get over it and would go on and on, asking, 'Why did it happen?' and 'What should we do?' I couldn't help her. She needed a professional to help her."

Karen Lee, Littleton, CO *Husband, Gerald, 52, suicide*

◆

"Don't say, 'I just don't know what I would do if Hank died' and then go off on a big tangent about 'I just don't know how I could stand it' and 'How I this or that.' It just reminds you of how bad it is going to be for you."

Ginger McLaughlin, Torrington, WY
Father, Joseph, 69, heart failure

Don't do things without asking.

"Somebody, we don't know who, came in right away and cleaned out our little girl's room and took away all of her things. We really didn't want that."

Sam Newton, Englewood, CO
Daughter, Deborah, 7, home accident

Don't offer to do something if you don't intend to follow up.

"After my father died when I was nine, I had three 'Big Brothers' [men from a mentoring organization that helps boys]. The first one wanted it on his resume. I poured my heart out and he was gone in three weeks. The second one was transferred after a couple of months, and the third one never called again after I got home from summer camp."

Joel Bershok, Littleton, CO *Father, Gerald, 52, suicide*

◆

"One of the worst things is not to be there or follow through, because it is another letdown."

Marge Lee, Long Island, NY
Son, Kenny, 25, killed by a drunk driver

Don't act like it's a burden if you're called on to help after you've offered to do so. You may not always be needed when it is most convenient.

"I remember getting sick at school. My dad asked one of mom's friends to come and get me. I sat in the waiting room for two hours, deathly ill. When she finally got there, she was so angry at having to pick me up she could barely speak to me. I felt like a huge imposition."

Carol Starkey, Boston, MA *Mother, Angela, 40, cancer*

Don't make a pass at the widow or widower if you are the spouse of a friend.

"When husbands of friends make a pass, it rocks you. It is so rude, and then you walk a fine line between showing them you are not interested and not making an enemy of your friends."

Donna Phipps, Lingle, WY
Husband, Lloyd, 39, cancer

"Don't treat the widow like fresh meat."
    Mary Voelz Chandler, Denver, CO
    Husband, David, 60, suicide

◆

"When your friends' spouses are making passes, it makes you afraid to call the very people you thought were going to be around to help you through the darkest moments of your life."
    Gail Lee Sander, El Paso, TX *Husband, Richard, 42, cancer*

On the other hand, don't assume your spouse is making a pass when he or she is comforting the bereaved.

"Don't assume that something is going on if your spouse is talking to the widow or widower."
    Dan Guthrie, Elizabeth, CO *Wife, Lisa, 30, suicide*

◆

"Suddenly you are a threat? Why?"
    Mary Voelz Chandler, Denver, CO
    Husband, David, 60, suicide

What to Do
at Work

Work can provide a welcome respite. Returning to the office routine, away from constant reminders at home, often helps distract from the grief. Even though I was still in a fog after Pete died, I wanted to be back at work because it made me feel more normal. The people there let me know that they understood my sorrow. I don't know how I could have made it without their help.

When I had trouble keeping track of things, the secretary in our office offered to write down everything I had to do the next day. She would hand me the list each morning. My co-workers were patient and kind when I would cry. Going home early or getting time off to go to the children's activities at school was never a problem for my boss. I was lucky.

Supervisors and co-workers who understand the grief process can help make the bereaved's transition back to work easier for everybody. Although stages of denial, anger, bargaining, depression, and acceptance have been well defined (check out Elisabeth Kübler-Ross's book *On Death and Dying*), it doesn't mean everyone goes through them in order, or only one at a time. Nice and neat they're not.

Most of the suggestions in prior sections apply to colleagues. Like friends, they need understanding and support. But there are a few issues that are specific to work, and following are some suggestions.

NOTIFY CO-WORKERS

It's easier if co-workers are aware of the loss. It's hard to have to explain what happened to those who don't know. Awareness of what happened also helps avoid uncomfortable, embarrassing situations all the way around.

"I asked the store manager to notify the people at work so I didn't have to tell twelve hundred people."

Ron Sentz, Midlothian, TX *Father, Mike, 88, heart failure*

◆

"Co-workers should be notified. You might think someone's been off on a nice vacation and say, 'Did you have a good time being off?' and the reply is, 'No, my mother died.' "

Emily Dickson, Phoenix, AZ
Father, William, 36, heart failure; sister, Louise, 47, suicide

◆

"When I went back to work and people who didn't know said, 'How's the baby?' I felt terrible for them. When they said, 'What did you have and how do you feel?' they had no idea how painful it was for me."

Susan Pottinger, Brooklyn, NY *Son, Jonah, stillborn*

Sometimes a co-worker who is also a friend takes responsibility to inform the office. If not, this task should fall to the immediate supervisor. If possible, it is best to notify people in person. In addition to the notification of their loss, ask the family what details, if any, they wish to disclose to co-workers about the death. Honor the request and ask co-workers to do the same. Remind them not to be nosy. Leave it up to the grieving person to initiate conversation about details. To this day I'm very prickly about sharing details of Pete's death with close friends, let alone fellow employees.

"The first thing I do is talk to the person who has experienced the loss and ask them if it is okay for me to share this. I then have one-on-one conversations with the people who are working with that person. Discretion is important. It's also important that everyone making demands on that person has sensitivity and compassion. I don't think the burden should be on the employee to go around and say. 'This is what I'm going through.' "

Carol Starkey, Boston, MA *Mother, Angela, 40, cancer*

◆

"I think it is really incumbent on the boss to send some kind of communication to let people know this loss occurred."

Seth Kaufman, Brooklyn, NY *Son, Jonah, stillborn*

◆

"One of the people who had worked for my dad for many, many years took his entire Rolodex and contacted the people who needed to know."

Francesca Amberto, Cambridge, MA
Father, Nicholas, 64, horseback riding accident

ACKNOWLEDGE THE LOSS

If you supervise or are in daily contact with the person, it's important to go to the service or home, say something, write a note or in some way personally acknowledge the death—even if the office has sent an arrangement or card. When the people from my husband's office came to the funeral, I knew that they valued him. When my co-workers and supervisor came, I felt that they valued me. It hurts if people you work with every day don't say or do something to acknowledge what happened.

> "When one of my staff loses a family member I attend the service. When the person is ready to return to work, I make a point to be there to shake hands or give a hug and say, 'I'm sorry. Is there anything we can do for you or your family at this time?' "
>
> Bob Buffington, Aurora CO
> *Father, Bob, 74; mother, Rose, 75, both of stroke*

"It's good when people from work come to the shiva or the wake if they can get away. When my mother-in-law died, a number of the partners in the office came down to the shiva. That was very nice. They barely knew my wife, let alone my mother-in-law."

Mark Cohen, Morris Plains, NJ

Mother, Rose, 33, hypertension; father, Abner, 85, stroke

◆

"At the very least verbally acknowledge what has happened. Say, 'I'm sorry to hear about your mom.' It's important to have some communication that isn't just business."

Jody Dutkiewicz Coates, Denver, CO

Mother, Mildred, 82, pneumonia

◆

"When my mother died, nobody at the office said anything. That was hard. Try to say something. Even if you cause tears, it's better than not saying anything."

Helen Coates, Exeter, Ontario, Canada

Mother, Marjorie, 87, pneumonia; father, Squire, 65, cancer

It's always appropriate to attend the service or gathering if you are a co-worker. If you don't know the family, tell them who you are and why you are there. Ask who is who. Don't try to guess.

> "A group came to our house and it was obvious they had no idea who the widow was. They didn't know me from a bale of hay."
> Mary Lou Williams, Scottsbluff, NE
> *Husband, Clark, 70, heart failure*

BE SENSITIVE TO GRIEF

Find ways to educate co-workers about grief and its stages so no one is surprised when the bereaved are crying, angry and irritable, forgetful, distracted, withdrawn, or depressed.

"Know that the person will have good and bad days for awhile. Explain that you understand and that it's okay."

Liz Stevens, Las Vegas, NV
Husband, Edward, 34, complications of AIDS

◆

"I think the sooner you can get back into something normal, the better, but if the person is stalled, I wouldn't come down on them. You need to be sensitive to what's going on."

Roger Drury, Burlington, VT *Father, Robert, 62, leukemia*

B e patient. Remember there is no time limit on grief. Although we'd like to believe the sadness quickly disappears, it does not. It's important to understand the memory of the loss is with us forever, and tears can surface anytime.

"A co-worker, surprised when a woman burst into tears at work a month after her brother's death, asked me, 'What's the matter? Did her other brother die too?' "

Ginger McLaughlin, Torrington, WY
Father, Joseph, 69, heart failure

G ive the bereaved time needed to begin to cope at work. A person in shock or too grief-stricken to concentrate can't be effective on the job.

"I am very fortunate to work for a family who said, 'Take as much time as you need.' I could go in on weekends and get my work caught up."

JoAnn Williams, Tillsonburg, Ontario, Canada
Father John "Jack," 69; sister, Lil, 38, both of cancer

♦

"My immediate boss said, 'Take as much time as you need as far as coming into work. Don't feel like you have to come in.'"

Darrell Proctor, Denver, CO *Baby, miscarried, eight weeks*

"I had to go back to work too soon, and was not capable of doing a full-time job nor was I capable of giving it the attention it required. It was not a good situation."

Gail Lee Sander, El Paso, TX *Husband, Richard, 42, cancer*

♦

"I ask them if they have had enough time off, and if they need more, I give it to them."

Bob Buffington, Aurora, CO
Father, Bob, 74; mother, Rose, 75, both of stroke

♦

"I wasn't an executive who could call my own hours. It would have been nice if they had trusted me enough to come in and do the essentials, then leave when I needed to."

Blenda Crawford, Littleton, CO
Sister, Cindy, 21, car-train accident

HELP EASE THE WORKLOAD

I'll be forever grateful to my co-workers who weren't angry because I wasn't holding up my end, but instead stepped in to lend a hand.

"As a supervisor, I say, 'A member of our team is going through a tough time. As a team we need to compensate for her until she can be at full throttle again. That may take some time. Communicate with me if the work is not getting done and we will figure it out. Be sensitive to the demands you are placing.'"

   Carol Starkey, Boston, MA *Mother, Angela, 40, cancer*

◆

"Offer to work for them so they can leave early. Offer to do things at work to lighten the load."

   James Bates, Denver, CO
   Father, James, 55, heart failure

"We were approaching a national convention and a monumental amount of work, but it was the farthest thing from my mind. My co-workers approached me, said they'd take care of it, and just jumped in and did it."

Theresa Soloma, Chicago, IL *Son, Dan, 24, car accident*

LITTLE THINGS MEAN A LOT

"When I came back to work there were flowers on my desk."

Donna Horstman, Richland, WA
Baby, miscarried, three months

◆

"His best friend at work brought an envelope that contained a collection they'd taken to help with any immediate needs I might have. Friends at work went through his desk and brought his things home, then sat with me to go over what was there."

Liz Stevens, Las Vegas, NV
Husband, Edward, 34, complications of AIDS

Suicide, Stillbirth, and Miscarriage

There is a myth out there that people who suffer these kinds of losses are somehow to be treated differently than those who suffer other types of loss. This can make friends afraid to come forward. They may not know what to say or be afraid they will say something terribly wrong, so they stay away.

The reality is that the bereaved in these circumstances feel the same way as everyone else who loses a loved one. They need to be treated in the same way as any friend who suffers a loss. It doesn't matter how or when the loved one died. The hurt and the sense of loss are the same. The grief is deep and lasting. Although it is important to be sensitive to what happened, the suggestions for offering comfort described earlier still apply. Let your friend know you care. Send food, flowers, cards, and notes. Stop by the house. Call. Check in often.

Following are some additional specific suggestions.

DON'T BE AFRAID

"People don't know what to say so they stay away. They are scared they will say the wrong thing. You don't have to come over and chitchat. Just be around. It is comforting to have somebody there."
Boni Fullmer, Casper, WY *Husband, Rod, 51, suicide*

◆

"Let your friend know you are there for him. Make yourself available. Don't be too pushy. Ask if you can come and see him, hang out, and visit with him. Tell him you would drop anything if he needs you."
Josh Strittmatter, Patton, PA *Brother, Jeff, 23, suicide*

D on't be afraid to express your condolences, just as with other kinds of death.

"If your friends don't say or do anything, you think they don't care. Say, 'I know how much Michael meant to you' and be there. Say, 'I am sorry I never had the chance to know Nicholas.' Say, 'I know it hurts and there will always be a place in my heart for them.'"

Elaine Reeves, Denver, CO
Sons, Michael and Nicholas, both stillborn

◆

"They weren't sure what to say, so they didn't talk to me. It kind of alienated me. Just talk. You don't always have to talk about what happened. If you don't know what to say, say so. I felt the same way. I was at a loss for words myself."

Loretta Cordova, Denver, CO
Daughter, Kathy Jenny, lived fifteen minutes

"We seem to have a belief that if we bring it up we will be reminding the person of the loss. The loss is always with you; it's a relief to know some people are willing to listen."
Janet Elsbach, Sheffield, MA
Baby miscarried, three months

DON'T BE NOSY

Let the grieving take the lead about telling you what happened. The family will tell you what they want you to know. If they don't tell you, leave it alone. Don't ask.

"What bothered me was when people kept saying, 'How did he die, when, why?' He committed suicide. I was nine years old. I didn't know why. The only one who knows is him. Asking, whispering, wanting to know was not helpful. All I wanted was someone to say, 'If you need me, I'm here for you.'"
Joel Bershok, Littleton, CO *Father, Gerald, 52, suicide*

"Don't ask personal questions. Trying to needle into the details of it is bad. I couldn't see why they could not understand it is a question forever."

Jean O'Hara, Cambridge, MA *Son, Bill, 33, suicide*

◆

"When they ask, 'Is your wife pregnant again?' I wish they wouldn't say anything."

Darrell Proctor, Denver, CO *Baby, miscarried, eight weeks*

KEEP ON BEING A FRIEND

Be yourself. Be willing to listen, but let your friend lead the conversation.

"Probably the best thing my friends did was to be normal. We went out and played golf like we always did before. They stayed focused on me as a person, not on what happened. They let me talk about it. If I referred to it in passing, they didn't freeze on me and say, 'Oh my God, he's going to talk about it.' "

Tom Stevens, Denver, CO *Son, Eric, 27, suicide*

◆

"Say, 'If you ever want to talk about it, I'll be here to listen, but I don't want to push you if you're not ready.' "

Rona Cohen, Morris Plains, NJ *Three babies, miscarried*

Reassure your friend.

"Tell the bereaved it is not their fault. I needed somebody to tell me that. This leaves a big, ugly burden of guilt behind—coulda, shoulda, woulda."

Ken Clark, East Stroudsburg, PA *Son, Darby, 26, suicide*

◆

"I felt guilty that I am alive and that I can find happiness without him."

Boni Fullmer, Casper, WY *Husband, Rod, 51, suicide*

WITHHOLD JUDGMENT

"Some church friends didn't believe she went to heaven because she committed suicide. They acted like it didn't happen and never even said they were sorry. I told one friend how my sister died and she could hardly wait to get off the phone. I never heard from her again. Even longtime friends really didn't call or talk to us like I thought they would. Some people think they can't associate with you because there's a suicide in the family. It hurts."
   Emily Dickson, Phoenix, AZ
   Father, William, 36, heart failure; sister, Louise, 47, suicide

Understand when your friend avoids painful reminders.

"I loved my friends' children and yet I finally stopped going to their birthday parties because it was just too painful."
   Rona Cohen, Morris Plains, NJ *Three babies, miscarried*

If you are unsure whether your friend will be uncomfortable being around babies or children, or if it's even okay to talk about them, ask.

> "You have to acknowledge that things are going to be difficult like showers or a bris. Find out what the preference is. Don't assume that because I'm laughing one day that I'm over it."
> Susan Pottinger, Brooklyn, NY *Son, Jonah, stillborn*

◆

> "My two sisters-in-law both had new babies. They asked if it was hard to be around the babies because they didn't want to make it harder for me. Actually it helped me a ton to see their babies because I felt closer to Nicholas being able to see and hold them. About six months later, it got harder, and I didn't expect that to happen. It's a good idea to ask if it's too painful to bring the baby along. Honor the answer, but check back because it might change."
> Mary Rindone, Omaha, NE *Son, Nicholas, stillborn*

Don't minimize the loss with platitudes, statistics, or simplistic solutions. It hurts when someone says, "Sorry for your little mistake" or "Just try to relax."

"Don't say, 'Well, you can try again,' or, 'It's better that it happened now,' or, 'Was the pregnancy planned?' as if that somehow changes the quality of what you're experiencing."
Janet Elsbach, Sheffield, MA *Baby miscarried, three months*

◆

"Doctors will tell you that twenty-five percent of pregnancies fail because something is wrong with the baby. That is just not what you want to hear."
Rona Cohen, Morris Plains, NJ *Three babies, miscarried*

REMEMBER THE HURT IS THERE

No matter how the person died, no matter how old the person was, born or unborn, the loved one is always missed. I will never forget how my 96-year-old grandmother on her deathbed spoke of her stillborn daughter, Ann.

> "I will always miss the people they were going to be. I didn't get to know them. There will always be a hole in my heart at graduations, proms, and birthdays. I am sad they never got to do those things."
>
> Elaine Reeves, Denver, CO
> *Sons, Michael and Nicholas, stillborn*

◆

> "Our emotional setup doesn't operate on any sort of a time clock. I still think about it at least once a week. I don't expect my wife to ever get over it. It might be ten years down the road and she won't have said

a thing, and she'll wake up crying. Who's to say when those feelings are going to strike? If I had any advice I'd say don't be surprised and don't think they're crazy because they do it. You might do the same for a parent or grandparent who died ten years ago."

Mike Horstman, Richland, WA
Baby miscarried, three month

◆

"I think it's pretty common that people think you will get over a miscarriage. But I will always miss my baby."

Sarah Campbell, Denver, CO
Daughter, Emma, miscarried, eight weeks

◆

"I don't think I will ever get over it, and I don't ever want to. Getting over her would be almost like forgetting."

Loretta Cordova, Denver, CO
Daughter, Kathy Jenny, lived fifteen minutes